Rhythms of Dignity

About the author

Akwasi Aidoo is a Senior Fellow at Humanity United, a foundation dedicated to building peace and advancing human freedom around the world. Prior to that, Akwasi was the founding Executive Director of TrustAfrica, an African grant-making foundation that works to advance peace, democracy and equitable development across the continent.

Akwasi's professional life in the last forty-five years has centered on human rights, peacebuilding and philanthropy. His previous roles include head of the health and equity program of the Canadian International Development Research Centre (IDRC) in West and Central Africa, head of the Ford Foundation's offices in Senegal and Nigeria, and Director of the Ford Foundation's Special Initiative for Africa. In 2015, he received the Africa Philanthropy Award in Tanzania.

Akwasi currently serves on the Boards of Human Rights Watch, International Development Research Centre (IDRC), and Centre on African Philanthropy and Social Investment (CAPSI) at Wits Business School at University of Witwatersrand in South Africa. He also previously served as a Board member of several international organizations, including Fund for Global Human Rights, Open Society Foundation's Africa Office, Open Society Initiative for West Africa (OSIWA), Oxfam America, Center for Civilians in Conflict, Resource Alliance, Crime Prevention Centre of South Africa, Africa Governance Monitoring and Advocacy Project (AfriMAP), Global Greengrants Fund, and Global Network Committee of the Ash Institute at Harvard University. Akwasi was educated in Ghana and the United States and received a PhD in Sociology from the University of Connecticut in 1985. He has taught at universities in Ghana, Tanzania, and the United States. He writes poetry and fiction.

Rhythms of Dignity

Poems

Akwasi Aidoo

Published by Amalion 2020

Amalion
BP 5637 Dakar-Fann
Dakar CP 10700
Senegal
http://www.amalion.net

ISBN 978-2-35926-100-4 Paperback

Poems in this collection previously published are on page 17, "Query" first published online by Pambazuka on Nov 21, 2006 (https://www.pambazuka.org/arts/query), and subsequently published online by How Matters (http://www.how-matters.org/2011/08/19/query-akwasi-aidoo/), and Thousand Currents (https://medium.com/@1000Currents/query-by-akwasi-aidoo-ef50b69f02a6); page 26, "Dreams of a Girl", first published in *Women, Men and Country: An Anthology of African Poems* edited by Khadi Mansaray (Createspace Publishing 2013); page 86, "In Peace (Or Pieces)", first published in *Twilight Musings* — an anthology edited by Howard Ely (International Library of Poetry 2015); page 88 "Dis-crime-nation" first published as "This-Crime-Nation" in *Poems for the Hazara: An anthology and collaborative poem*, edited by Kamran Mir Hazar (Hazaristan Press 2014).

Author photograph by Martin Dixon

Cover artwork by Adeusi Mandu Mmatambwe. Lacquer color on masonite, 60x60cm. Used by permission, Wolfgang Bender & Jutta Ströter-Bender Collection.

Cover designed by Anke Rosenlöcher

Contents

Africa-Wise

Rhythms of Memory

Not So Be It

Meditation Pauses

Africa-Wise

The Vital Signs Lay Hidden
(For Ayi Kwei)

The vital signs lay hidden for centuries
in our memory's defeat. Are they to blame
for all those times we killed eating teary
salt? When the tiger in our soul lost
its Tigritude to the deal-maker? And we lost
count of how long the rain-maker had slept?

The rain almost came when that wind of change
cooled our red hot eyes. And the rainbow flashed
a black for its first completion…Then, in our moment
of fear clad as black power we forgot to save
our dear Lumumba.

With freedom our last word,
that first step we needn't have
begrudged Madiba the priceless "Akwaaba"
Losing no love for that "Castle" of defeat
as Cabral too was cut and
the stump became the tallest tree
…in our shrinking forest.

The silence had been long,
showing all there was no fluke to
our borrowed ways of death.

Then, the rain finally comes,
fading our trenched doubts
and casting a glimpse of
The Beautyful Ones, a few healers
Slowly
Quietly

Reaching out
        Seeking
Vital signs to
D
     E
        E
           P
              E
                 R   meanings with
Surer beginnings,
Firmer bearings…

This time,
not the defeats,
not the defects,
nor deceits.

Only steady work,
shared work, loved work
till the crust gives way
to our bridges
to the future –
Our crassless future
where the signs become just
plain, normal. And
Solidarity has no other name
called betrayal.

Spread Our Wings
(For Kofi, Atukwei, Niyi)

Spread our wings
                    you say
and flee straight
the breast of the earth
scorched, to touch the ceiling
wailing that the sun can't
dry or shine.

        Shapeless
when it fits us to take
flight, Valley Stream
            meandering,
the showers of
shokolokobangoshi giftologies you
spray and pray lift us
easy beyond the SunShowers
but to where?

We don't know, but one thing.
Our rhythm rhymes
by apt logarithms —
African   People's   Time
from 19-Kojo-Hohoo…

When it suits us to take
flight from the base,
AptPower raises in our way.
We go
        we go with no strings
attached, not
to the destination
except
to humanity, all of it.

They Said…

First, they said
"It's all in the Color."
But then the whole world went Creole
So they said: "It sure must be that big
family thing." And when the Irish showed
size had nothing to do with it
They said: "It's the Brain, you know.
Something called IQ."

Then we invoked Timbuktu
and the Pyramids, quoting
Bernal and Hunwick and Davidson
Still, they said: "They're simply too slow."
But thing is we kept running
and winning both sprint and marathon
And making mince of their languages

Now, with no answer to that and
No body parts left to assault
They say: "It's their National IQ."
We say: "Learn just one of our languages and
Then we can talk."

Seasons
(For Odia)

Seasons it takes for
A shower of dreams
Our vision of courage
The shared smile
Out of our open sores of anguish
Memories of defeat, and withering petals
To dance to the call of Nananom

Seasons of unceasing *asemboni*
Then Brother Marley wailing
So our souls waking
Walter and Martin before him
Making clear we shall overcome
Then, seasons of more wars, hot, cold and silent
The tallest trees even felling – Patrice, Amilcar, Eduardo
      Ruth
         Steve
           Samora…

Still, homegrown seasoned combats
Steeled to tame Kwaku-Ananse acrobatic minds

That season of cretinous dealership
Mobutu, Siad, Doe, Abacha, Bokassa, Amin…
And the outcome…

O lest we forget the season of SAP
Making us "See And Pass"
Signposts to life and love
Twinning warlords, con-flation, globalization

Still, they offered more seasons of pedo-gangs
Of fecund armory and Rambo dreams with
Pseudo-revolutionary fits
Worthy only of resolutionary passion

Now, this season of fervent pleas, old as hell
To turn birthright to pawn-right
When our songs of rainbow bid Naija-rise
We, your people, plan to win love
With Madiba drawing sweet smiles on our battered faces
Which you, the Flutist, ready for another melody.

Query

We are a developing country   you say?

That we need
Time to mature?
            Unity to develop?
                    Discipline to compete?

Hmm…when we have
Time
Unity &
Discipline

And   before we
                Mature
        Develop
and
Compete

Can we
Dance?
Dream?
        and
Struggle?

Can we resist your
folly?
With justice?
Can we?

Our President Made Us Proud

Good evening, our people.
Our President made us proud today
In London, Paris, New York, and Tokyo
He laughed with Kings
Danced with Queens, and some gangs
In Berlin, Washington, Singapore, and Rome

He dined with the rich
Saw the Pope, amidst a chain
Of commanding guards, with no smile
He pleaded forgiveness
Of our sick debt. Sold our National Plan
For Progress. Unveiled our budget

Then signed the big Global Declaration
On Death to Terrorists
Winning, toasting the health of poor nations
Dining at the best restaurants, he chopped sweet
Food, and oh, he shed no pepper-soup tears
For our pain.

Our people, our Viral President
Made us ProudLess today and for evermore.

Please Come Back Home
(For Natalia Kanem)

From the point of no return
Through the clutched hell-gates that
Birthed our memories of spelled glory
Please Come Back Home

From the sixth time
Of circular dance at the tree of forbidden life
Where we said you must go and forget
Please Come Back Home

From the claws of killing time
In gulfing passages of wailing waves
Armed with the stubborn sense of struggle
Please Come Back Home

From your silent songs of sorrow
In soul-massaging blues
Naked in all those razz-matazzing jazz
Please Come Back Home

From where the sun's sudden defeat
In cotton-rains of winter seat
Your undying dreams of life and joy
Please Come Back Home

From where you walk in millions
To claim bits of freedom to be
When Mi'Lord says you can
Please Come Back Home

From where the warm spirit dies
In bloody cold climes of faceless lies
Where dreams of Zion are deferred by dismembered limbs
Please Come Back Home

From the placid pains of Babylon
Where love is short and hatred long
So short and long they forget the name of fragile peace
Please Come Back Home

From where your love dies
In lightless alleys of Triple-K drenched blood
Where no one, but no one, hears your call in grief
Please Come Back Home

From all these and more,
… Our Love…
Please Come Back Home

In Our Harvest of Triumph

In our harvest of triumph
this lean season
of gloom, we gather
no tears of revenge
at those who for centuries
took our pride of SunScape
We will softly rub Karite and black soap
in the scabs and scales of
anopheline bites, scooping
off your back, and
singing a wake-up song, not
whispers of stolen breath,
to our forgotten
shared boat called
Humanity.

Conakry

Long
>   a refuge for Afrikan sheroes and heroes;
freedom fighters:
>>   Kwame, Amilcar, Mariam, Stokely, Mashinini
and more...

It's all over now
>   over before any liberatory fruition

these days it's a dig for GNP
>   symbolized in 3-piece suits
>>   and grand billowy boubous
"très chic" they say
>   all in the service of SAP

African Unity?
>   Sorry, in the hands of policiers and gendarmes
>>   stiff as wood, and bloated
worth penny a piece for entry.

Mogadishu and Dakar

Walking away, he said to me:
> "We're a coin. Africa, we are a coin."

Not sure what to think,
I'm sitting here thinking:
> Some spirit must surely explain these things

when nothing else can.
A decentering amalgam of tongues
could have shaken the armor of the other, but it's not
> broken.

One armed to seek the face of God
here and now; the other seeks alms and faith in
work, peace, work. The one with a multitude of
neighbors has women running the streets and markets;
the other with street-lords pushing women
> subaltern.

The pride in culture is the same.
The spirit of leadership, is it, in one?
The spirit of dealerships, is it, in the other?

They are at the opposite edges, with venturing spirits
that give back, going by:
> "I can't live there, I will give there."

The spirits must converge.

Ankober! Love...
(For Bahru)

Ankober! Love...
Our hearts, for your balance yearn
In the rhythms of power & dignity
You blend our soul, blood & destination

The fog you shower on us
At the summits of Imemihret, Figre Gimb & Gorgo
And in the Great Rift Valley
Says you care for all humanity

Never mind our stations in this life
Low or high. And if your scenery
of Shoa memory is taken with pinches of
blessed sacramental salt Aba Massayas brought

To the strangers' Gate
Yesterday, today, tomorrow changes not
How the curious & mighty fell at your feet
Let Marefeya showed that to Count Antinori!

From Liberia with Questions

In this beautiful, green, wet land,
the war is everything.
Everyone and everything is named
by a single question:
Where were you during the war?
What happened to you during the war?
Did it happen before or after the war?

The war had its life, they say;
it just happened to people.
The war did things to people;
people didn't do things to people.

That's sure what happened.
The war ate its compradors and victims.
Everyone scorched by it,
some deeply, many their lives.
But not everyone went with its logic,
for some with courage went against it.

And, here I'm,
a total stranger,
sitting on the balcony of the top hotel
overlooking the roaring ocean
that couldn't silence the ever-running staccato of guns
nor the shrill screams of their victims.

What do I know, I kept reminding myself
as I stumbled upon facts, new and old,
which spoke to the unspeakable brutalities,
memories of which facts alone couldn't express
beyond the gaze of their witnesses.

Dreams of a Girl

My genderless dreams of ascent won't be
deferred by teen missteps that have filled my body
heavy, shaken my brain into turmoil, stricken
my heart with anguish...

Not the dream of my own sweet embrace
of books bigger than my head and
schooling beyond the limits to create shades
of dignity for the stuck poor

Not the dream of a future without nightmares marring
the will to grow out of the trough under eaves
named poverty, nor dreams yet unborn to ride
the indomitable spirit the ancestresses bequeathed

Me to go the path from Sa Lone to the ends of
the world in peace and freedom for all girls and
to read and write in poetic license to the summits
of Fourah Bay with pedestrial anchor on terra cotta

My genderless dreams,
trong lak morning batu, won't be
deferred now or ever, for nothing
but nothing will deter me!

As You Go, My Friends

As you go, my friends, go
sweetly, tread steadily
On this long walk, please go softly.

Stretch, as you do your hands, widely
to laugh, to live, to give all there's
to share; to share all there's to give.

The moon, when it shines
on your path, may it show that you cared
that you were here, there, everywhere.

And, the rain, whenever it pours,
you'd know the gods have blessed
your gentle footways. So go on, my friends, go on.

The angry winds, those of Juba,
they will not shake you, they must not
shift your course past the pathway of the gods.

And, the skied Capes of Good Hope,
on any day, may you see them and from them,
through the vintage to a mist-less Robben Island.

The birds of Nairobi, the stones of Makerere even
may they sing to you in whispers
of the endless universe.

And, the mysteries of Addis, those of Kigali,
when you encounter them
may they urge you on this quest for beauty.

The strutting fireflies of Kinyeti,
if you find them vying with the stars please know
that they too want you to see the gods shine.

So, go on, my friends, and sing
on, as you go like the best into the future
please go on for those yet unborn.

Your voyage then, rain or shine,
will be named in discoveries of
life, light, love and peace.

Fragments of Struggle and Sanity

I. Odoba

I made a quick dash
for the gun, I knew
a dash was the only way
I could, but they didn't know that.
"Easy. Don't shoot"
the fat soldier said
with outstretched palms
fanning at 180 degrees ginger-speed
then sheer power over uselessness

The uselessness of sheer power

"that's of no use"
Something said to me
Then the fat soldier looked
past me, his lower lip twitched
a little sideways
his moustache looked whitish
against a ray of sun
his upper lip like he had swallowed
more pepper and a little salt
and before I could say Yaa
he was on his knees
shot by the wickeder who wanted him silent.

II. Marcus

Work, work, work
Eat, sleep, taxes
Bills, shh till
You die

There's nothing
you can do
Nothing you can do
man
Joe, ain't that so?

III. Talibé Kid

On the streets, I pause
to size up the rich and poor
and ignore all those beyond
the shadow of certainty.

I plead in sheer whispers of dignity:
Cast your stream bangles of death
around my Dream Pit
Scare me not with all the prayers.

IV. Somalia

Out of nothing
came the idea
that we must
never forgive the
light of daydreams
that gives one
language of harmony

V. Greeting

Here we greet in tongues
of shivering ripples –
How de bodi?
Bodi dey for cloth?
Shitting well? –

Greetings are the window to the heart
They knock on the door to harmony
The way we say:
Make love, no war
The first words

After God said to Adam: "Be"
and before the devil said to hate
Greeting after greeting
after greeting.

VI. Our Spaces

The spaces we carved of thick stone walls in
our love-ridden stupor as birds of prey
chirped away their death anthems are now free
my love. They're open uncavey spaces
covered by aromas of Cabo Verde
salsa that carry the spirit of African souls
you said went away to Bahia beyond
the boiling waters when steamers of our
bloodied laughs disappeared. Today we
do not allow them to make gutters in our hearts.

VII. Money

Money rules
with a soft sledge look –
spenders, sellers, seekers,
stealers, fighters, speakers,
liars, beggars, gifters –
its hand hidden
in the pores of our dreams
not in their skin. We pray for it
we spray it when it floods.

The root of all sin?
Not when it smiles on you
and shines your eyes.

VIII. *The Alien in Front of Me*

I'm sitting in a hut-restaurant
face to face with an alien
with a face that says:
Why aren't you at my feet praying like all?
"All" are the poor
poor with no choice but bow
before this alien with no shade
of smile when a little girl comes
with a rainbow and offers gentle palm.
Ah! Wait a minute!
He's laughing loud with no smile alert.
Just burst out. The alien.
The little girl is back with a flower.
He was looking for love.
This alien.

IX. *Addis with Love*

In white I sat against the leopard
against the bogolon dead-end skirt.
"Some mocktail, please"
I sweetly ordered
as the fatigued-dress Oyinbo marched in
with the Guru bard in slow tow.
"No mocktail today." Only strong stuff.
What the heck, scale me up.
The red wine worked wicked ways
on my brain cells, and
the AU walls went up some more.

X. Cheese in the Air

Cheese, delicious cheese,
delight of the lens,
captivating, eye seeking all 32 teeth
or what's left betraying residues of white or yellow
cheese with crackers
when smiles crack joyous and
sweaty glasses crackle across seats.

Tomorrow's Gain

Tomorrow's Gain
      will come unbridled

when the Soul-Lock breaks
      and the light of struggle

turns gloom to bloom,
      with your break-away moves, and

a new beginning of seeds planted,
      impossible yesterday,

      as sure as the joy of a dream
comes true or a chance not hoped, and
      your light of struggle
        turns gloom to bloom,

and
today starts
with a break-away idea, with
new beginning of seeds planted,
impossible yesterday,
unshackling our wings for a
      Free Africa!

Bearing Witness on the Pathway

I am the single lonely bird
long perched upstream
      silent.
I've seen all the pitiless happenings
to our living dead
long accustomed to the one-way path
we've come to know too well
      as death
but whose appeal we know not to resist.

I've seen all those who went
never to come back.
I've seen those who went
      not knowing.
I've seen the path in its glee and shine,
in its gloom, partial and total.
I've seen it dormant and devour.

In all its appearances,
the path leads treacherously
to the crocodile stream.
On one side lies the swampy quicksand
into which stranger thieves of our dreams
were always chased.
Back then, only such ugly souls
were chased that path.
      Not anymore.
On the other side lies the rocky hill
from where the devout contemplate
the crocodile god
the god of destruction
disguised as savior.

The quicksand never fails
in its consumption,
and the stream always lies
at the betrayer's end.
The rocky hill looks deceptively innocent,
and there is no denying
   the power
of the wicked stream.
No one who goes on the path
comes back.
It is betrayal itself,
the surest way to destroy one's own,
and the quickest passage to suicide.
No one knows how the path came to be,
but everyone knows where it starts,
   for it is home.
No one quite knows the alchemy
of its destructive end,
but the few wise ones among us
say it's worse than death itself,
especially death from war.

We well know those who walk the path
never become ancestors.
This is not the way life continues.
But somehow,
this terrible path has become our way.
Many were betrayed by it,
many still are guided by it,
although its deathly end
is forever certain.

For seasons on end,
this path to the terrible unknown
brought pretty nothing
to those who moved lives,
even beautiful lives,
by it to the point of no return,
and none of the multitude
that kept alive its bloody shine
fully understood its bitter end.

In time,
the path created haunting shadows
and demons uncontained
all these years.
It nurtured mighty trees
with deep roots underneath this earth
that has carried millions to joyless ends,
while no one ever said Amen
to their silent songs of sorrow.

The path continues to shine
from the blood of the devoured
set against the constant flapping rays
of the sun,
as they talk sweetly about its glories.

There is no talk of its past
lest it would seem
the voices long silenced by it
rise to dement minds.
So the path attracts like never before
and holds few mysteries
beyond the minds of easy believers.

Here's to Africa Day!

(For 'Taju)

Some say "African Unity Day"
Some, just "Africa Day"

Whatever your choice,
here's to a freer, safer
united Africa of our dreams!

And, let's re-member
our dear Taju. The broda who chose
this day. He spoke words with spirits
that grew and stayed longer
than the Baobab, inflamed our passion
for this land, spoke truth to power,
unveiled leaders who are dealers
in dream-sale, made history.

The broda who ceaselessly said Never
when a fake yes was a sure path
to our woes, wane and wail...
Here's another, to Taju!

Egg Africana

It's the same look. From the rugby-shape, yellow
Yolk, rich dark brown, snow white, small patches of
Uneven shades with oviduct blessings
Upon closer Inspection. Not at all
Like Africa, pistol-looking as Frantz saw
And called to our radical mind. It's got
Africa all over it, though. The layer
Embraces earth fleshing it out gently
After the finger rectally explores
Its imminence, then nestled-detention
With full meal privileges. Before, the
Layer roams neglected in the backyard
Hunting insects, specks of wild grain sprout in
Savanna-scape, until a few trappings
Of guinea corn for fingering ends its
Freedom. The egg survives a day perhaps
Then ends in a pot on three-legged
Mud cooking stove with ashy smoky fire
Not a cold poultry section shelf in wait
For a total stranger. Here, it's straight to
The pot for Bossman. For kids and women
Christmas must first arrive. Once in a long
Moon though the layer revolts, scratches a
Hideout beneath the fruit tree, and releases
The egg for a chick or a wily snake.

In the Land of the Escapees

Like a lonely ant sat I in the midst
Of the music cascading into the sky

Then a lonely, happy bird descended
To the ground some ten feet from my right foot

It quickly picked up a drop of something
Bread crumb perhaps, a piece of cake, even

Bird dropping enmeshed in bits of sugar
From a nice cup of tea or chocolate

Pancake that some lonely escapee from
The north may have ordered in this

Enclave of gyrating hips. There sat I
Alone with a copy of Heavensgate

Heavensgate! My escape land too. Then I
Started thinking about Chris Okigbo

Chris! How even his end was remarkable
Like his lineal endings, his choices, his

Style, like a star that seemed to lose its way
When it shone brightest across the oceans

In all this darkness. But did he really
Lose his way? When he took such Biafraic turn?

Or was he the full moon that lit the darkened
Heights of our gloomy hearts, silent mindset?

Then the mass, "Le Carol", my bar tender
Informant called it, broke my thought of Chris...

Escapees, holidayers can't go to church and have fun
At the same time, he said, as if to say:

They're here for sweet sin. A little prayer
Helps to ease the guilt of the escapees.

Africa Arrival

As the flight come landing, over the statue

Family, applause, laughter, waiting with

Rituals of libation and drums rising up

Incantations of blessings touch the sky

Centuries of resilience come alive to say

Africa is alive, will live, must rise again

Rhythms of Memory

My Mother's Song

My mother's song flew
with melodies of silence
day after day through
the ceiling of the Harmattan clouds
     sketched
in rainbow stitches of harmonic pleas
and fell back streaming tearloads
of naked memory.

Singing for life

her notes went a long way
to the beats of our hearts like
the southern sun breaking
     out through the clouded sky
except for the anguished spaces
in its ancient rhythms that said no one
but no one can tame the Griotics
of this scorched earth called home.

Mama

In fifteen years, you bore ten
In five, you lost five. The rest you carried. Healed
When the tiny mosquitoes floored them

When you created food, always sweet
We could swear by the sweat from raging compound
Fire, if not by your steady feet that waddled through
Reptilian rice-farm swamps, stumped
And survived the sun-charred wasteland
Legacy of the oil champions. For what prize?

Your headaches were evidence of witchcraft
Your pain faked, they said to spite the marital-rival
The new young one he has lost reason for. Yet

Too much horror sightings caused the blindness
That drained all tears of pain and pride. You rose still
Beyond the root-depths of woe-manhood
When rain stormed the heat, silence reigned
In my heart for you. Fear went out the window where
Demons lurch in wicked gangs and

You still stand, stride in dignity across the earth
As we, who defied the fangs of death. As even the
Destroyers cast their sights low and give way…

To You!

Anti-Rio-Cism
(For Brad)

Everyone said, as I came searching,
that peace is your lost memory
and hate the serial killer of your dreams.
That all shades are mere white and black,
the alphabets in reverse, and you live
in denial when the rainbow strips
your summits and valleys. That you wag
one-color tale of glory, and another of defeat
even as your soccer team is a unison of hues.

Then, I came. And these I saw…

Sunny-radiant skin, smiles and miles of rose-hearts
silky hair, kinky hair – most black, a few
geriatric grey, all in harmonic sounds on
black and white with godlike gyrations I could
swear by Mama's foot came from Ouidah.
Sounds that moved hearts and shades of brown
to each other aiming, it seems, for the summit icon.

And, then, some more…

A chameleon chain of defiant dreads
to paper-thin lips in slit eyes to twinned-gourds
in rhythmic steps to songs of joy Yoruba-born,
syncopated with Praia-swings mélanged into
a globalized arc in Lisbon, Paris,
Geneva or St. Louis, who knows
…and, massaged some more in
the sweet sweat-bowl of your Favelas...
The dawn gunshots and waves-silencing wails.

And, then, I wondered…

Yes, the waves-silencing wails
from the mountain holes across the street
were sharper than the Sheraton wake-up calls
spewing into pathways of black and white blood on
red hot macadamized streets.

But by sunrise, the colors rise again,
…and through echoes of ringing pain,
a smile-wielding sage, a born-again activist,
in Che-cap, runs to disarm the ugly.

Then Peace is here, jumping on its way…

When I Encountered You

When I encountered you
You were said to have fled
But you spoke no words of fear
Your pained eyes shone through
the lens that should have healed
our short-sighted vision
of "country broke, country no broke,
we dey inside!"
It was dead night in
sweaty Asankragua
Where the solitary oak
by your abode still bore
witness to your strength
Spirit, Soul

Then, silence

The meticulous old keeper remembered
it all as I sat contemplating
Your whispered absence. He spoke of
        The softness of your voice
        The generosity of your soul
        The tenderness of your steps

When I encountered you for the first time,
Your exile was nearing
the first of its serial endings
And your unforgettable name spelt
Freedom for our Nsawamites

Then, you returned
Just when the dawn bells rang to start

The feverish music whose
wavy dance we still must learn
After all these years of no sweetness
here… You brought more
revered wonder. You spoke
little as though your soul bore
Our heavy-duty burdens
Or was it the weight of our un-civic discourse?
Or the smelly odor of our unforgiving
politics? Still, like merciful rain
on our long-parched soil, you came down

Then, you joined Asamando
And as you did, I too left
To understand, to seek the vital
links that join our worlds together
Theirs and ours, across oceans
Yours and mine, across times
Your exile was my holiday
But I understood, with time
I understood the meaning
of your sacrifice, I understood…

For a Rights-Full World
(For Randy)

With your rhythms of dignity
and sounds of care, the togetherness
of your amazing soul and spirit
you trailblaze ways of grandeur.

Forever expanding the frontiers
of our ever-thinning world
from America to Zimbabwe – into

The Rights-Full World of
humanity untied and united, you show
the courage we need to make it, own it
and never trump it.

You show the journey
as treading from the Kill-Bow state to a
RainBow World with One Parent.

We will follow your way on
the quest to disarm the Wall-Lords
of our world of countless nations
with your unalloyed bounteous harvest of

Rigor
    Anchor
          Nimbleness
   Dignity
Yearn

Meandering never.
Sharing ever.

Bearing Peace with Grace
(For Nomfundo and Khaita)

Nana often said:
"Future," she called me, *"You must*
know this Divine truth...
The unalloyed spirits of beauty
with sense and sensibility is
when you sport peace,
bear it in rainbow colors in solidarity,
stand up, bear with grace."

So, *"Sporting, Bearing, Standing*
with Peace in Garb and Grace", are
the wisdom words I always dream
for the beauty and sanity often
rocked by hurricanes, Tsunamis, quakes,
distress and inequities unleashed
by graceless destroyers of nature and peace.

The dream is fed even more now
by a *Nom* with a Womandla *Fundo*
standing in full glare of humanity
and mirroring nature in its glamor
of colors in rainbow offerings.

Keep bearing on with grace
with firm feet towards the future,
hands embracing wood and earth, and
eyes saying, *"Shall we smile, strive*
solidify, synergize for nature and peace?"

Your bearings speak louder
                    than a thousand words.

Here, Womandla! For Peace and Joy!!!

Reed on Yankee Freeze
(For Ihonvbere)

Against the odds, you should not
have moved. Not beyond
the nightmare
station home became.

The wind would blow you
to easy silence, if luck struck,
they said. But move our dreams
to birth...? No!
Perhaps only where merchants of
kwashiorkorist fate defend the nightjar
curse which is here
not there

We who know the journey
know you defied destiny and
scheme to make all know
your destination is not now,
and not here
where the ignoramus struts wicked
pride as only
an empty drum can
sound. We, your voters-in-waiting,
make this pledge: that when you call
we will say: "homeland or death!"

Closing the Gulf
(For Dattatreyudu & Rosalyn)

The news came across
the Atlantic echoing the oceanic
sounds that drowned the dreams
of trafficked middle passagers
of centuries old, flooding the cerebrate
with cascading sounds
between disbelief and the why-me angst.

Closing the gulf was a bridge to Global City
of melanged India, Philippines, Russia, America
and nameless more visages safely spaced
behind scrubs of eclectic pieces, V-necked
for love Hippocratic-ally oathed,
bouffant-shaped cloth cap, latex gloves
closed toe-shoes to boot my cancer cells to pieces

The pivot of it all, as I gyrated
uncontrollably, were two great souls:
anchoring the pellets for the epic battle.
His gentle smile caps a global acclaim of perfection
Her warm care bequeaths happiness.
Together, they pulled back my trust of life.

My Son's Questions

This morning, on the way to school, my son asked:
"Dad, why are those men working in the heavy rain?"

The rain has been relentless and so have been his questions
"They don't feel the rain or what?"

I took another look. "It may be easier for them to dig
When it rains the ground softens up."

It didn't work: "But, Dad, they don't even have shirts on."
Finally, time for class analysis.

"Son, they probably have no choice. Must finish today's work
Rain or shine, or they suffer more. See, a bit like our watchman.

"He never gets to sleep in his own bed five nights a week
That's life, son. Life for some."

"Yeah, it must be hard."
Silence. Long silence pregnant with more questions.

"But, Dad, can't they say no? Won't they get sick from the rain
Beating down on them? Who is their boss? He must be wicked."

"Well, son, their boss may even be a regular Dad like me
With children he loves, and also helping lots of poor people."

"So tell me, Dad, why can't he
Whoever he is, help these workers?"

"Well, he needs them to work so he can make money
To pay them, support his family, and help other people."

More long silence, then the tearful punch:
"It's not fair. The rain is beating them."

Cornered, I turn to education for rescue
"Well, son, let's look at it this way:

Those workers probably have little or no education
Because they dropped out or their parents had no money

to send them to school. So you must continue to work hard
At school. That way, you won't end up like them."

"Still, it's not fair"
More silence.

"I have an idea, Dad…"
"Yes, what is it?"

"You know how I say I will be an animal rights lawyer
when I grow up? Well, I think I will be an animal rights lawyer

AND a workers' rights lawyer. That way, I can defend people
like the workers in the rain."

"Great, son, that's great!" In a split of a second
My heart flashed back to my glorious youth!

I Have Arrived
(For Lilla)

I have arrived
in a world I was told needs to laugh
more, even if I landed with a scream –
a scream I designed to knock down its walls –
walls built to imprison love –
love of humanity by humanity

I have arrived
with a sharpened tongue, not in cheek,
to scribble new words of courage
to firm up everyone's grip of Grandpa's plea to
     TERMINATE
Life's amputation by bellum spree

I have arrived
armed with a detective nose,
not poking shaped, to smell out all
the Unyokeristas Grandpa & Sissie
curate to unleash the promised land
of Pacific Giants with pertinacity

I have arrived, I, of the Beautiful batch

with ceaseless will to open up
your hearts to spare the forest
and animals and children and
the old and stones and all else
that exist and must exist for humanity
Békét hozok!!!

He Went with a Goodbye

He was a loving father, though he had none,
In the afternoon he said goodbye,
    he went
to pick up his ten-year-old son
from an after-school activity and died

A suicide bomber-bee ended its life
with a stink to his left shoulder. It hurt but
    he brushed
it aside, screaming then laughing
to embrace his son. The welts grew
his breath lowered… Before he could say
no to his son's, "Are you ok, Dad?"
he was on his way to the ancestors

    He went
With goodbye… I braced myself for life.

Home in Exile

In the land of exile
a million émigrés linked
their souls fettered, festal.
Musing, flustering or blasting
they affirmed each other and the struggle
home.

They invoked the spirits
of lost epics to retrieve
the vital links of love to harbor...
from a haunting past to forge dreams of new
home.

In the land of exile
where memories of mortgaged triumphs
written off (in)delible sweats
of hate and love soured
their spirits grew from gifts of life
from those who, not knowing more
than their humanity, gave home and more.

Some Words Stay for Life

Some words stay for life
with great joy. As tiny windows

from the past into the future of our
dreams, they are priceless gifts

of compass and anchor
together equipping us for

lifeboat. Like when John said to finish
the meal serving for the same at a

minimum always and when
Ama said it's OK to give a life

for a life saved and a friend mused:
"Life has a life of its own and it's long…"

Fontomfrom
(For Henry)

Fontomfrom…, Fontomfrom…, Fontomfrom…
the drums sound from home
the end of your sojourn marooned
in the Diaspora that had become home
announcing the beginnings of your worthy entree
to Asamando

the drums reverberate from afar
the endless list of your creations on par
with the very best of our kind so far
announcing the conquests for your sacred exit
to Asamando

the drums solemnly declare for all
the chain of prizes to come for work we so adore
to build our pride and confidence again and more
announcing why your belonging is already assured
to Asamando

the drums sound again and again your teaching and
inspiration, the films you created for life and pain the
people you touched and changed, the vision you said to have
announcing for all to hear your honor, humanity and journey
to Asamando

the drums thunder for the last hour
telling us to take heart and sing for the life we gained
from the tallest tree in our forests at home and abroad
announcing to Nananom that you are on your way
to Asamando.

Ilé-Ifè

(For Falola)

Ilé-Ifè
rain and sun love you
to life with united shades
of Falola – our esteemed
lasting gift of Olodumare per Òrìṣàs.

Riding with Joe

Joe arrived earlier
Thank God
I must catch the 6 am train
He picked me up several times
We always talked light. Today, it was more
than light. It was real fun talk

"So how you today?"
"Can't complain It's a nice day out"
"Yep! It's lovely, isn't it?
The sun is out and bright. But this weather
can't seem to make up its mind
One day it's good, the next it's freezing cold."

"It's supposed to be nice and warm tomorrow."
"That's good. We're one day into spring, aren't we?"
"Yep"

Silence, as I call in to check my mail
Message is indecipherable
Sounds like a call from home
I can hear snaps of Twi and nothing more.

Joe makes a sudden stop at the light that never
seems to go green for anyone
I look up and out, and Joe is nodding
with a tiny serious smile at a middle-aged black woman

on the sidewalk. It's a pretty common gesture
among Black folks, I reckon
but it refreshes my imagination:

"Do you know her?"

"No…"

"Among Black people all over the world…"

I speak slowly and see Joe straighten up,

taking a quick glance at me in the rear mirror.

"…Among Black people, there's something

so beautiful about the way we sometimes acknowledge

each other in public even when we don't know each other."

"You're right, brother. It's solidarity, I think."

"Yes, and it's beautiful"

"I agree"

"Now, what I don't get is why they gave us

the shortest month of the year, February

I mean why can't we have a whole full month of 31 days?

Know what I mean?"

"I get you, brother"

"And I'm sure they never asked us to choose.

We won't have had the coldest, shortest month

of the year. We'd have gone for the warmest,

longest month something. Like August.

That's what really bugs me."

"I see your point."

"Besides, why can't we have two whole months, anyway?

Two whole months, can you believe that?!

No way they gonna allow that."

I made it quick for the train…

"Take care, brother!" he waved with a wink.

In Search of Today's Meaning

Racing around in pursuit of
today's big meaning like a horse
champing on fertile grounds of antiquity
I land on the back of the Atlantic
spirit to space with little to offer,
it seemed

A crafted cranium greets me
in Cosmo Text. The TV blares
away with Davis Cup 2010
play-off Harmonic blurts from
a jukebox incite the ears.

A Pente container
holding no signs
of strategy contents
has its frontline, relaxed

Chairs on top
of chairs. Other attractions
of no mean meaning…

A Gabonese children's dance
teacher in French
accent, tender world
music soothing the nerves
from flux, books and
books from nowhere
in particular. Happy noise
upon noise rise
in crescendo. The air
conditioner is at perfect

temperature in this hot humid
presqu'île of culture-mix.

Alex, the boubou-garbed
bartender, offers
a cup of Espresso with
"welcome to our world!"

To Act Sweet

Sometimes, in the corner of this
Grand station of the never-eaten
Apple, I want to act sweet
to a complete stranger
I mean like stretch out my freezing palm with
true smile, say good morning as we do
with full eye contact and ask
how all the family is doing and
if the body walks good
and how the day is going and if the children
have eaten and if sleep came deeply and if
the enemies are tired and
whether the rivals have been silenced
by shame yet and how
the last funeral went and who took the
children of the departed and
where the state stood on it.

Who knows how a complete stranger,
in this endless stream of lonely crowd in
matrimonial bliss or whispering curses with
their cell phones, will greet me back?

So I drag myself along always
undisturbed by law enforcement
until I stumble upon a brother from home
and scream Akwaaaaba!
All in a stubborn dream that lands me
in a spot with full glares shooting at
360 degrees for public disturbance.

Random Brother

In the elevator the other day
I met my random brother for two short minutes.

With the same Lands' End suit, same height
it seemed. The Lord was his barber too
He said hi; I said hi. He held the door
for me. Placing him like a long-lost gem
in Senegal, I thanked him with smiles and
one word, "*Merci.*" He said two: "*De rien.*"
I went to a corner to think, when did we
last meet? He said, "What a heavy downpour!"

I said, "I've seen nothing like it before,
not here." He asked of home, then heartily
told of his first time there, Ghana. How
a cab driver so undercharged him he
wanted to settle. I said Senegal
was good too. Here, they will negotiate you
to earth or them to it, all and all in
joy, if you know how. Same spirit laughter.

Then the elevator came to a creaking stop,
with a bump. We shook hands. Then, "I'm Karl from
Accompong Town, Jamaica, By the way."

And he was gone like a dream, leaving no trace
but imagination of a long-lost brother.

The Birth of My Twin-Heart

Saying goodbye was leaving half my heart.
It all started that dawn when you decided
to pot my toes in the garden
of your soothing palms
That dawn, my brain went to work
like never before. "Potatoes", the word,
woke my brain cells,
watching you pot a toe, one toe at a time, in tow,
one after another at a patient, thoughtful pace,
with that sweet cream whose scent I thought
I smelled some 20 years before
during those storied Arabian Nights
in Zanzibar when I'd go seek a shadow
with a soul to commune about why we must
inhabit this preposterous world of greed
spewing out of control, against
our fervent struggles to share.

That dawn, my twin-hearts were born.
Then I thought: which twin cracked
the twin joke of "Go Wild, Have Twins"?
Frightening, confusing, I thought.
And then I thought, why not?
My heart of twins means this is for real;
that this is unchangeable;
that this, the gods have joined.
So, yes, I too shed a tear, not as prodigious
as yours seemed from that snaky queue
to that home-land security check,
but long enough a tear for me to know
half my twin heart was in your warm bosom.
Need I say it again, my love?
That I love you?

Re-Treat-Ment

I flew all the way here
        Wondering.
     Then I came and these I felt:

        Treated fairly with exchanges of respect
and goodwill. Humanely communicating
with myself and the invisibles of life.

Touching and massaging nature with self-healing
     from years of anguish
about death from this earth.

Yep!   I've been re-treated
     Unyoked, Refreshed
Re-Treated-Mentally

Beyond measure
and this life
at this rebirthing Re-Treat.

Coronavirus Carers

Your bouquets of care
saves sanity in this time
of sadness and fear.

Your social presence
unites our humanity
against destruction.

The unalloyed care
and the bounteous sacrifice
you give shows you are:

Makers of forest
out of the trees dispersed out
into organic

life of trust and faith
with pure solidarity.
Your legacy lives!

Our Deathless Nana

I was ready to cry out loud
when Nana planted an irremovable
smile on my face as she lay
on her death bed at 95 years.

She pleaded for celebration
as her Honam, the parental body gift
had witnessed so much beyond
measure before its disappearance.

The other two elements of her, like ours,
can't ever disappear she said.
Her Sunsum, the Divine gift of soul
her Nkrabea, the negotiated deal

struck from Divine dialogue
before parturition, are her legacies
of indefatigable passion, always on
display even spheres of sheer darkness.

Celebrate! Celebrate!! Celebrate!!!
and let go this overworked body to rest...
Nana interminably urged with a
beaming voice vibrating her death bed

Her Sunsum and Nkrabea, the twined
collective assets will stand out
for joyous display as her Honam lay
in a pertinent conveyor artifact that

bears witness for countless generations
of transformational Voyagers, Dreamers,
Change.

Our Time Is Human
(For Tim)

One day, on a philanthropic ride
To The Presidio, I heard you think this:
Listen. Time is also Human
We're twins. It moves. It changes.
It can be good or bad when it wants.

It shines and darkens
Storms and steadies
So tell me: Can we stop
Finding and keeping time
And let it be like us?

Finding and keeping time
Like an arrested criminal when
It does no wrong?
We don't own Time so
We can't say my time or I gained Time.

Time is never lost. So, let's bond with it
As twins, not to trigger angst with
Our distant cousin christened
Space except when we traverse
It with Time majestically.

A Naissance of Our Love
(For Ema)

A naissance of our love you are:
Our Cohortful hearts yearned for
your arrival in balance of rhythms
of power and dignity.

The fog you fantabulously evaporate
from UncleNet in the "*Aha! Moments*"
Across Porto summits and valleys

say you've come to sooth
all pains to end
our sorrow in this crazy world.

You've come with a smile
not furor and, pray, say to
those who choose to belittle humanity:

"Bow before me – the betoken
courier of Love you've wronged
by eating the morsels of peace for breakfast."

Philanthropically Speaking Suzanne
(For Siskel)

Years ago, when we met in Africa, I searched
for the mnemonic that would engrave you
in my Ashantified brain.
The word Philanthropy begged for inclusion,
for diversity sake, and
the prename, just and compassionate,
reflecting your soul, yielded to a Hyphename.

It is a marriage beyond duality and binary;
it is the spirit of your gentle soul,
the soul of a spiritual amalgam that says
      philanthropy without social justice & peace
is like the globe without the glow
      of shedding light and warming hearts.

A questing bird…
      with firm wings of Javan proportions
and the wind behind sails that
touch around the globe,
You've stayed here long…
      far too long,
for your spirit to sprint on
to life's ceaseless callings.

Yet, how would we have been loved and left alone
in the absence of your pure prodding
      and steering hands all this time?
How would we have survived?

Your marathon was the breath we needed
to craft this identity, this vision
        for a golden twining.
You gave us time and fame
        We give you this name hidden in our hearts all along...:
        Suzanne-Thropy.

Ode to Social Justice Philanthropy

Social justice philanthropy
Philanthropy for social justice
Social justice in philanthropy
Philanthropy in social justice...
We know thy spirit, thy soul inspires us,

But, what art thou? Who art thou?
We seek thee, social justice.
We dream thy magic.
With tears, we command thee, philanthropy,
lift up thy head out of the silos, come out,

come out for social justice,
for us, the people without heirdom,
stolen or earned.
Come out, social justice philanthropy,
for thou art needed

in Zimbabwe, in Burma,
Somalia, in South Africa,
America, in Russia, everywhere
In every form, we have created thee,
debated thy features, what levers, we ask,

And, we ask: art thou systemic change?
or structural rupture?
Finely garbed?
Maloccluded mess-dramatic?
But then again, who cares?

Really who cares,
whether it's the frozen-face VP
Or the swaggart-bland Oga smiler?
Who cares?

When You Left

The sun is shining. The hurt is still there
but it's a new day. Someday, when it ends,
I can say this:

When you did a U-Turn, I died
to know what more there was to know
Reality turned a new leaf of fiction
The world stopped, my world spun nothing
steady. I embraced my pillow hours
mourning the one thing I could hug
and find the next morning

Then one morning, there was no more pain
Left in me. All gone. As though I was dead
I staggered to the bathroom and looked at
my face in the mirror. I saw a smile. A smile
like the sun. Gentle, glowing. I spoke to it
"Is this the change?"
"Yes, move on beyond the memory", it whispered

I went back to my writing desk
straight from the mirror, my face unwashed
how does one wash a smile that has come
after time and time of pain, throbbing pain?
I turned on the computer, looked through
the meadowed window to a slim branch
of a lonely tree. A colorful small bird was perched,
chirping away some repetitive melody
Not a bird person, I looked harder
It flapped its tiny wings but stayed
It, too, seemed alone.

My computer flicked, a sound came through
it was time to get to it. I proceeded
to delete. Everything. Deleted. Everything
Left no memories. None.

And the smile came back and
With a wink said, go on... go on...

Dream and Peace

Slowly you drew out my dream
You urged peace and joy
You held out laughter as lifebuoy
You said we could dance
Till our eyelids collapsed with sleep
And our souls merged in shared sweat

You always came with a smile, sweet as sin
Sometimes with eyes cast low
And coyness that spoke to the firm soul
Defying even the hieroglyphics
Sometimes as a jumpy deer
With ears wide for melodies of the spirit

True, I failed to love at first sight
For nothing in me had a memory of trust
Beyond the moment.
Betrayal was all I knew
Not companion, definitely not reciprocity
Or tolerance of the little strays I pleaded
Calmly I stepped out of my shell
Which protected me, as well I knew, from hell

Gifts always come bearing birthmarks of betrayal
Still I managed to trust and dream
And stepped out into your rain
Embracing you like air, wanting a fresh start
I gathered gifts of love for the wind's destination

Why?
The tortoise would ask nothing less of the fox
That always sends her back
to unshared breast and warmth

Then the end came, as it always does
With more questions than answers
More pain and silence
About these things of trust and hate
Compassion and betrayal
These things that make and break hearts

Still I refuse to seek alternatives for
I now know no cure for destruction and hate but
Love and peace.

Strands of Dreams

I. Lost and Found

When your quivering lips
Embraced the sensuous
teeth of this breast of earth
with captivating eyes
and told of joyous
puerility, my love,

it was the handiwork of
the gods come home
to this time
this space
all our very own:

to share, to shape
as we dream
for peace, for pride
as we aim
to the galactic
cyberspace of stars for
sight of this pained earth we
lost and found.

II. Looking for You

How did I find you?
From where it was all broken, I searched and
Searched for you, fixed down like a beaver
Escaping the glare of the high-beam lorry
Mimicking the split skies
Till I came upon the mares of the hut
They burned down, all ruined,

I slipped, fell, face up, eyes dim
Calling the angry skies for a ray
Any light. Any light, I murmured.

To a soul full of rain... Then there!
There you were, among the chosen
Few at the kingly table.

Then I touched you, and with you
The way home shone, firm even
In the torrents from the angry dark
Skies that my prints on the ground defied.

III. In My Soul's Eye

In my soul's eye, I sit
With my palms facing
the stars... My sights on
that day, that blessed day
When you and I will step into
the gods' smile arms locked in
our vintage love, cropped
In blessed marathon showers

Now, I sit here
on this narrow night
patch that will cede
to our shared bed, ending
the fountain of tears that
Drown my pillow
each
lonely night.

IV. Love-Chain

I love you, Dad
     I love you, Son

I love you even
when you're mad at me. Well,
I'm mad at you...'cause I love you.

I love you not
because I'm mad at you

I know... It's cool
Love-Chain all the way round.

V. Aging Love

The clock rings five
Slowly he pulls the cover
off his head. Eyes red hot
from sleep he has plenty. His woman lies
in another room. They loved
each other but were long
past when nights flourished
all-laughter of sweaty love
broken by slips
into depths of sleep till
good morning came smiling.

VI. Ma'Mira ChuChu

The first time
when the cold conspired with the heat
to lock our arms
bearing whispers of love

And the second time
when the quivering lips answered
to the migratory mole locking
our palms in warmth against
that gossipy wind
and your captivating smile said:
See, I can still love!
as I preached
with no gaps for laughter
And the hug
when my heart said:
Here's a cave for my homeless love.

VII. Sitting Next to You

Sitting next to you
in the sky, when the signs say I may be
heading to the village of no return

Is it the gift promised
undelivered at ground zero
when the sunshine pales
for boomerang

Is it eternal
Love unknown…
Unmet at ground zero?

VIII. In the End

In the end
When he died, his sentence was
    Four short words:
"He loved to death."
And he died happy.

Not So Be It

In Peace (Or Pieces)

Comrade, since you say
We can't eat democracy with
All those sour choices
Pinstriped lies
And decorated fools

Since you say
Only war will do

Tell me then –
How else can we dream in peace?
How else?

Can we dream?
In Peace?

Together We Will Walk

Together we will walk
    side   by   side   warmly
swinging arms in Arecaceae grace.

Crassless, classless raceless
we will walk together
gently, silently, firmly,
uphill to the vaults

Where ancient mysteries hold
memories reposed, exposed
of our triumphs and shared community.

Tread and thread. Up and down.
Side by side. Back and forth to dream
out teams of teams.

And there is nothing more
to it than that. We will walk
together, palm-in-palm, unpegged

by what long strewed shared dreams,
to a world that belongs to all who live in it
with Peace, Love and Trust.

Audacious
            Boffo
                    Composed

We Will Talk, Walk and Work Humanely

Dis-crime-nation

We move in clear voice together
With verse metered to the heights of Hazara
Pain and lodge this poem-plate loads of
Justice against batterers of your dreams and

We move on this-crime-nation to account
On account of stretches countless in cutovers
Marked by limbs of Hazara dignity kidnapped and
Massacred timeless in fashion steady

In lands -*istan* and -*an* where faith, peace-named,
Calls but denied for dogma traded & maimed
They try & try… maiming dry and you cry… but
We cheer your rising spirit on the endless lands you share

We salute with hands clasped the wise
Ways in your dignity & spirit even when your smile
Is robbed in full view of our naked eyes & ditched a mile
Deep beneath their troughs of dis-crime-nation and pillage

They condemn you, the irrepressible kite runner, but
We, the PoemTeam, sprint across oceans
"For you, a thousand times over" and declare:
Beyond dis-crime-nation, the Hazara shall rise again!

A Poem No One Will Care About

Looking for inspiration today, I'll write a poem
no one will care about. A poem that says

nothing about the State of Africa.
It won't be an ode to our great faultless leaders.

It won't be a sonnet about stolen elections or
An epigram they can say

maligns them, declare seditious and ban
with impunity. Not a poem street children can devour.

Or one to unveil the trafficking of humanity & illicit flows
on the dusty roadways in the labyrinths of our SoulScape.

It won't be an elegy about a girl raped, stoned dead
by law enforcement, or curtain-raise the mirth of the war-lords.

It won't be a poem the post-modernists will
interrogate. A poem the praise singers won't love.

Not an epic poem the newspapers will publish and pay.
It will be a poem that won't bring tears

of joy or pain. It will be a forgotten poem
about nothing that stands in the way of our memory loss.

On African Soil

You can't believe this, m-e-e-n!
there we were
      21 of us
             straight from Babylon
                fried but fired
finally made it to the motherland
with tears in our eyes
         laughter waiting
silently waiting to break out
Full of excitement
      you could touch
             before fruition
Then, Bang!
    "Les blancs d'abord"
this on afrikan soil? Shoot!!!

(Dis)Spell Power

How do we (dis)spell power?

Fire
      Ire
Brimstones
      Stones
Fear
      Ear
Distance
      Stance
Hate
      Ate
Pass
      Ass
Entourage
      Rage

Daily, they spit

Fire and shower
Brimstones to birth freaking
Fear even from the calculated
Distance they swear not to
Hate as they see and
Pass us with their Griot Crass
Entourage

We resist with

Ire the
Stones they cast to the brim of our pepper soup and from
Ear to ear we whisper to gather our movement nuggets in

Stance against the mounds of hope they
Ate empty like termites. Stirred, we offer no rat's
Ass with a Tsunaming wave
Rage is how we (dis)spell power.

The Clown Baobab of Bandia
(For Anta)

I am the Clown Baobab of Bandia
In this colony, enclave, reserve… well
Call it what you may… but in this land of
Indignities I am the sole one
With my dignity in hand and
Measures of laughter to hoot/boot

I am the Clown Baobab of Bandia
I stand slanted, half my roots in the air
Calling on the sauntering lizards who come
From a thousand and one places to kiss
My ass. I thump my nose flat at the angry sun

I am the Clown Baobab of Bandia
I invite monkeys to bare their tongues. To piss
In my mouth for your camera. My unfisted palms
Holding high half the sky from your head
I declare in thick lipset:
I am the Clown Baobab of Bandia.

DonorSpeak

Ladies and Gentlemen,
We the philanthropoids working
for a World Without Aid
are gathered here
today at the Super-Hilltop Suites Hotel
in search of a new paradigm
that will enable us to catalyze
a unique, innovative and strategic
partnership-based affinity group
of like-minded funders to philanthropize,
leverage and aggregate
our investments for unleashing
sustainable development
of African entrepreneurship
in ways that humongously debunk
the notion that indigenously-owned
and propelled initiatives cannot go
to scale and/or move on
their own steam effectively
efficiently and ecosophically
without phalanthropoidic fostering
through our FAPs.

Any questions?
                        Silence…

Power Lords

Here is their first class
Lesson: Never forget
To impersonate joy
Instigate passion
Infiltrate the beginnings
Of their modern prince, then
Defoliate and de-root their petals of life,
Intimidate their seeds of courage

Better yet...
Fabricate a few snow jobs
Of melodies of Trojan proportion
To humiliate their best
Interrogate in jest (if need be)
                    Then...
Invade a few
When passion seizes
Mutilate a few more
For tomorrow's unshaken fear,
Castrate that head
Of timeless dreams of joy

If they persist
As cockroaches do...
                    Then
Our good people command you to
Assassinate the brave
Exterminate the weak
Terminate the young
                    And old at once
Annihilate
                    And

                    Annihilate
Extirpate them all...

And, if still they
Emancipate the future
And intone Ubuntu
Songs of love and peace...
                    Then
Sweetly invoke law and order...
For the sake of the senseless State.

From Where We've Come

We are the cream
your Praise Force command scooped for the pedestal
of booklong wordship that awed the predators.
Fat cats we were not destined in our field of eligibles
         but promised when
your fattening beckon call came. No,
you were not alone in urging us to go;
in the marooned dream chambers of our cultures,
we well practiced our flight as prizeful as midnight
Harmattan love songs we chirped for the chicks at
                  sundown.

Our flight was on a witching broomstick
borrowed from nowhere. We made it,
spurred by a future spelled in pride of place
heated we knew how by our juvenergy.

         We flew. In droves,

we survived
the nerve-deep degrees of epileptic temperatures.
         We learned
the ways of silence and wind-shaped salutes of hi.

We came to accept looking elders in the eye
and skipping as much in strangers
were the paths to safety.

We saved our joys and sorrows for home.

On our return, fear and hope is all we've got.

Nothing

The Spartan wings of nothing swipe
a monster green, a bleeding blue even
a blinding white

when we ask to see the ramparts endowed
oceanic bosoms of raving sounds
before our doom,

that quiver stiffly.
Each time, nothing shakes
our fervent palms for mercy.

Each time, those memories of defeat
just look us straight in the eye and spit
mushroomed angst worthy of nothing.

Each time, our dream fires stretch, and
the forked tongue doodles fresh, and
the mystery flash dies a little.

Next time, please, next time
Bring us a song soothing
to warm our souls... to wake our battered shells.

Power-Full Question

How you begged, palm
In palm, smiles swinging
Wild on your knees:

Please
         Please
                  Give
                           Me
                                A
                                       Vote.

                                                    Now,

                                        With
                              Stabs
                    You
            Are
      My
Curse?

Graffito-less

Alone it stands, not just
soulless, untoward, rising skybound
On a clear day it stands
against hanging vain-strutting smoke
passing as leftover clouds
claiming its own airspace.

Before us it stands
Alone, tall and treeless
no shrubs either, only concrete
slabs hiding no messages coded
for seeing minds, clairvoyant eyes.

This rise, erected
into our soul pock-marked,
announces fretfully
"Hurl-'em out of the way!"
This rise, etching a hurried boom
in our doom, stands to say:

I dare you
I was, I am, I will be Graffito-less.

The Past

Still

the past sits
by our pains-plate
like a crow waiting to
eat the carcass of our dreams.

And tear-streams of gathered debris dirge

our freedom songs and rival a river
flow of reborn vision aiming for
the mountaintop against the
fury of status quo

Stillers.

The Crusaders

Our tragedy this
>   Fall
Is counted in thousands of dismembered joy
>   And
Discounted in caved vengeance with smart bombs.

The faithful on that side sang:
"From their caves of Adullam to ours of Afghanistan
We take our stand
From Saladin before to…
The Fearsome Genius (permission to speak in your presence,
please)
We sought only a little destruction, a few mangled hundreds
perhaps
But Allah gave us Destruction Unlimited…!"
In honor of
>   Broken
>   Dreams,
splintered feline pipe-dreams in large quantities
>   dreams too nightmarish
for our age of fundamentalisms

The faithful on this side sang:
"From our crusades of Jerusalem to theirs of Kandahar
We take no prisoners
From de Bouillion before to…
The Brave One (Nostradamus's prophecy)
We sought only handover justice, dead or alive
But, God! He gave us Justice Infinite…!"
In honor of
>   Broken
>   Defenses,

Polished oversold pedestal-defenses in heavy penal quantities
              too unjust for our age of impoverishment

Between them and the War
They forgot the truth of
The pounded mountains
        into valleys of ash
The widowed woman-child
        of invisible visage
The thousands disappeared
        without chemical trace
The ocean-tears of the globe
        for a people sacrificed without shame
The Snipers of youth
        with but slings of David
The child-soldier specialists
        of amputations to cripple free choice
The Generals whose medals and boots
        shine of blood and brain cells
The Corporate Citizens who "had no choice"
        when our beloved Ken was hanged
The guns and diamonds they've come to value
        so much our schools die
The 47 million without health insurance
        in this land of plenty.

They forgot to whisper that
        each bomb, smart or stupid,
                is no respecter of rights, but

Between them and us
They did not forget
The little humiliations:
Profiling and threats

So fear is contained before all else is tried
Justice denied before its infinite possibilities
Laughter eavesdropped before it infects all
A cough forbidden before treason is born
Voices silenced before they numb common resolve
Identity encased for peace sakes
The efficiency of military tribunals…
They did not forget to giggle-dance how
rights can go to hell
Alarming even Safire

And this
Winter of (dis)content
When terror
Breeds
Acrobatic bombs
Bleed
Collateral damage
I see the cold-warrior with
smitten smile and wide wink saying to
the evidence of Nostradamus' prophecy:
      "Way to go (un)Great One!"

Do They Still Dream?

In the middle
of the great ocean
          Souls stoop
Blinded where none
visits them.   No One.
Do they still laugh?
          Do they still
love? Do they?

These people, who only swim in
dream, do they still
on the narrow patch
in the great boiling waters
the great invader calls
backyard?
His bloodied muggy backyard?

Do They Still Dream?

Katrina & Povertina

One lousy day, came
saddling Katrina hurling abusives
at Povertina. All saw it somber,
and none merry made
safe the perquisited Shrub

silvered over with dough
recalling the joyous days of old
he'd storm Inaville
to have too much fun to see.
Blind then as now to smoky-garbed Povertina

As for the high priests, who in quieter times
father our nightmares,
they kept their deafening silence
in the face of the tumult-Ina bash
till vying Rita showed up to steal their NapJoy.

Sandy

If we had our way and say you would come
as a lover you would come to sooth our

pain to kill our sorrow you would come with
a smile, not furor and you would say to

those who choose to belittle us: Bow
before me... But now, you come against us

like an angry goddess we have all wronged by
eating your totem for breakfast.

What She Got

With spirit vast and heart sweater than honey, she asked
Little for need and much to offer. To let all her children
Live and make the middle passage just
When the call of adventure came. To understand

She wanted no more than to be left alone, free
If not loved. To accept she's different only
Not sightless from some Helios-tort of ridicule beyond color
From Phaëton's platonic skin-deep embrace

To sing enchantment to all who came, arm in arm
With the wind before change arrived and meaning
No harm but peace even to those with dreams
Of enslavement sold as manifest faith of redemption

And what she got was a damn
Shot in the back with a change of name!

Languescapes

The numbers don't lie
In the one languescape we
The brains of state and anti-state
Share

With the grand masters of yore
There is no room for masses
Without refinement of soul
In Fela-langue, it's
Dem-all-crazy, littered

With a merciless sole tongue
Not for masses that speak in tongues
Of Mother Earth
Their earth. The masses say
"Oman panyin"
"Man hiie nyiel"
"Du Kplola"

And tens of it in variance
We respond
"Follow Citizens"
"Peaceful elections"
Our speeches are eagles
Aimed for the sun god

"We're hungry and angry"
The masses say

And we say, "We are
One Nation, One People, One destiny"
Within justice designed

For constitutional guarantees
Of state security
Period.

At the Doctor's Today

The receptionist again...
It felt like a kick in the back,,
if you ask me, she just won't let me
forget that I need a little health
The last time, it was my broken jaw
from a little brawl
with Stanio in the local bar on Main Street

Today
A mother of five, still expecting
walks in like a millipede, all five in tow
And an old man, so alone like
he's come for company, snail-walks in
and makes magic for the youngest of the five
with fingers that haven't grown beyond teenage

Dr. Broadhead walks in
like an eager priest to whom
all have come to confess the latest sins.
I belch, pretending, turn to the New Yorker
looking tortured from abusive readers.
Something in it says "Eat Cheap" and
it's got French fries, pasta and meatballs all over it
"Eat Cheap, Die Hard", I imagine

Final check-in: an odd couple
Who sure have come for a check before
A Florida vacation they can't help themselves:
Hi, says the Nurse (out of the blue),
Someone got married 'oer the weekend
Woman: *Oh, that's nice!*
Man: *Yes, it's Joe Stilho*

Woman: *Oh, that's nice!*
Man: *Had the callous for years, right?*
Woman: *Not for years*
Woman: *He married the same girl he was going with, right?*
Man: *I don't know*
Woman: *She was such a beautiful girl.*

Dr. Smarthead calls and I ran
I'm in the hospital for lunch today.
I will do an abbreviated exam
Ok, I submit body
Oh, it's BPH, he says before confession
Nothing to worry about, he sums up
rubbing the stethoscope's kidney lobes
that serve as a poor rosary
And, that was it for 100 bucks!

There Was a Time

There was a time when the lights went off
they felt safe. It evened out the darkness

for them and the thieves. Their tears did not shine
for all to see. The moon and stars sparkled.

The strutting gang had to wait, limped tight.
The pen-robbers went into lull, full-state.

The children played
hide and seek. Equality loomed in

ways the MDGs could learn. Now
when the lights go off, all hell breaks

loose. The generator of noise kills
the sweet rhythmic sounds of tropical rain

drums on their corrugated iron sheets
drowning out the Godly nightcap lullaby.

Zero-Sum Game

Zero is both the provenance of our growth
and the end point of our eternal rest
and steadiness. So let's value it and
end playing games with its identity
today or tomorrow, year after year.

The zero-sum games aren't fun, as per a
San Franciscan homeless man who opined
questionably thus: "If we, the worthless,
have only zero sums then why do those
Billionaires have countless zeros in their
net-worth figures?"

Means they stole us, right? Or
Nicodemusly borrowed us with no
Interest, crassly making us indebted?
We got to get our worth back or forever die.

Talking to Myself at Six

I came to this world with a clear creative spirit.
Then started the journey that the earlier arrivals
Have put me on: "Say it this way," they say.
"You understand?" they ask. "Please sit down,"
they implore. "No, don't do that!" they order.
"You don't like the food?" they question. "What
did you learn in school today?" they demand.
"It's time to sleep," they command. "It's time to
get up, Baby. Time to get up!" they repeat.

When I'm daydreaming for the good of all in
a socially-hazardous world, it's a nightmare —
"What's the matter? Are you Ok? Why are you
looking so sad?" they interrogate with a saddened
face. When I sing in my head the lyrics
I brought with me at parturition, they're curious
with hardened faces: "You finished your home-work?"
And, if I open my mouth with an inquiring mind,
It's: "What made you think that?"

Inside me, my curious spirit refuses to bulge
and assuage my mind, which sadly feels renamed
"Inquisitive" and is going petrified, with these
final words: "No worries, Dear. You are good!
Keep going on the creative path, Great One."
It brings so much joy and meaning to my heart.
"Look at that creative spirit,"
I will say from now on.

Naana Sage on Coronavirus

Naana sage shares now
With hindsight, insight, foresight
Corona's esse:

Yes, its time has come.
No, it will not hike forever.
It will slide with care.

Pause and pause isolate.
Pause alone together, please.
Don't pause in-person.

She says it will skid
as humanity sprouts in
sense and sensibility

Co ro na vi rus
won't end our joys forever.
That much we must know.

Meditation Pauses

Nurturing Earth in Quietude

In pensive quietude,
Let us nurture Mater Earth
with bouquets of care.

Let's wish, imagine,
coagulate our new-found ways
to hug Mater Earth —

Bearer of our lives
with trees, water, soil, and all
we need to survive.

Mater Earth draws breath
from meditative offerings
with wise passivity.

Let's wave Aloha
love with our zephyr-sound hearts
one beat at a time —

B e e p...
B e e p... B e e p...
B e e p... B e e p... B e e p...
B e e p... B e e p...
B e e p...

Time Pause this Season

Time pause this season
Bestows wisdom sounds from Earth
to connect with each.

With eyes closed, deep breath
the invisibles are seen
and our spirit comes home.

With our mindful pause
quality time and life spike
in meaning on Earth.

Our time pause bestows
gifts of nature
we see with eyes closed.

Up the Heights

Let's stroll up the heights
with a bee yakking sweetness
to ears yearning

Weaving through the curb
of metal in tricolor
with our beloved dog

Watching to create new
ways to bop the obstacles
this crisis hands down

Still we sit, hugging
sanity and life streaming
hurriedly to us

And the sun will set
ample shadows of smile to shine
curvy paths to peace.

Let's Stretch Out and Pull In

The sun and the moon
up there stretch out in turns for
harmonic beauty.

So must we stretch out
to lives outside us, known or
unknown, near or far.

For peace and freedom.
For self-care, love, sanity.
For meaning of life.

Let's pull in our weight
from the heavy load crisis
those at the subaltern level
carry day-by-day
with no salvation.

Let's pull in our noise
and silently listen to
the humanity in us that
yearns to be heard about
the dots and stretches
that connect us all

in physical distancing.

Let's pull in our angst
from the politricks, so our
dreams triumph for a world
that's leveled for all
to traverse with
steady peace and pace
from this crisis.

Living Deep Is Deep Life

Living deep is deep life.
In all times, "living deep" has one simple meaning –
Engaging with the down-trodden to deepen their lives.

Deepening lives is different to each
but the connecting tissue is the same –
Finding joy from sharing lives, wisdom, and smile.

Makes us live deep, energizes
the spirit in us and enables us to see life
on this earth as beyond the limits

of crisis losses or constraints
to the limitless gains of
life, light and love for all of humanity.

The Belt Warmed My Hips

The belt warmed my hips
The dawn the snowfall
Welcomed me to the unforgiving

Land of enchantment song. The one
We learned to sing
When the candles would die and

The birds would chirp away
Our last goodbyes to our stolen dreams
In sleeplessness. My hips, then, only knew

The rhythms of soft dance and love
and worked itself for it.
The belt warmed my hips down

To the last breath.

Lompoul Sand Dunes

Lompoul Sand Dunes
I'm in awe of your breath
Time winds
Here for millennia roasting
Rusting, resting
Crusting Wind blows across

Sahelians in distances
Defying voice and word

Why settle here? I
Wanting secrets of chance?
Destiny? Will? Which?

Why live forever
When nothing does
Good or bad?

Peace, Conflict and Harmony Questions

Does Peace come from Conflict
or from Harmony?
or come from both?

Does Conflict kill Peace and
Harmony resurrect it?
In time spread out on its own?

Or does Harmony conceal Peace
and Conflict exposes its concealment?
In no shred of gameless contestation?

How can we enable the agency of peace
as the simultaneous sanitation of Conflict
and deconstruction of Harmony?

Or is this all a bunch of tyranny of concepts
from those pontificating for honorability?

Letter to My Invisible Ancient Friend

Dear Invisible Ancient Friend,

Season's greetings again!
And welcome to my time and sphere.

The brightness of this day
Has given me the golden opportunity
To share with you once again the journeys
Of my lives, and to thank you most
Sincerely for bearing with me and helping
To retain my integrity.

In my first life, I was a crocodile
When the great Tsunami
Happened ten thousand years ago,
I came back as a branch of a tree
In the forest of sanity until the
Gargantuan earthquake fell me
To the ground with the risk of
Consumption as firewood by the
Old ones, but I retained my crocodile
Shape, spirit and senses until
You chanced upon me.

You bore with me and agreed not to
Reshape me even as you sought
To polish my semblance for meditative
Engagement

So, here I celebrate!

Your sincerest crocodile-nity
With break-less limbs!!!

Today

Today. It rained. It shined
its headlights.
It came and left long.

With a balance of shades
and the valance of its own
decorative self.

It stood out against all
the bullies and naysayers
of humanity itching
to start their shakedowns.

At its end, today made them
spray and pray to no
gallantry or reputable end.

Snapshots

I. Punctuated Peace in Rhythm

No peace poem today?
No, **Peace,** poem today!

No peace, **Poem**, today?
No, peace poem today!

No peace poem, **Today**?
No peace, poem today.

II. Poetic Notes

Dear mine, on terra firma I am still anchored
Beneath it not yet, for our work is not done
Nor above it, where I dream to be sooner
So wind and machine can swing me across
The ocean to see my darling sister
Before the frying & crying season
              That violates
Her skin, cedes to the falling one
              That foliages
Our spirits in renewal.

III. Dream Big

Dream big to shut all
gates against a nightmare small
or big sneaking up our wall.

IV. How Do We Know?

How do we know nobody knows
an unwelcomed fact or truth
hidden from the purview of all those
who can see with their naked eyes?

How do we know those who know
what we don't know about those who
don't know what we know?

V. Future

Future must be in existence even
now, as our parallel universe. Our quest
must be discovery and engagement with
Future with no strict assumptions but with
open hearts and minds – to find Future as
our hidden selves; and distilled perfections
and imperfections mirrored all over
our visible universe; as unending
nourishment of our shared souls and spirits.

VI. Turning Gold Into Dirt

In our Holy Villages, they've come
avowing to turn dirt into gold, but
truth be unveiled, they turn gold into dirt
Polluting golden opportunities
assets and dreams that transcend ages
and ages of transmission.

VII. The Clouds

The clouds gathered for
Rain to spray on the Sun-day
We prayed for shower.

VIII. *Come Up for Air*

Daily, may you come up
    For air by walking, singing
        Dancing and laughing.

IX. *Sounds of Redemption*

Beyond and behind
The disruptive noises of
Humans, redeeming

Sounds of nature from
The birds, wind, sun, leaves and stones
Brought life back to me

In that moment of
Despair.

X. *In Plain Sight*

The contrasted shades
Of color in nature are
Beautifully aligned –

Depicting how non-
Antagonistic forms of
Contradictions get

Deconstructed and
Synthesized very sharply
Dialectically.

XI. Touch Wood

I am a stick for
Uniting humanity
With diversity

Balance, Equity
And Alignment – all from same
Source birthed by Relish.

XII. Stretch Out

The sun and the moon
In us stretch out in turns for
Harmonic beauty

So must we stretch out
To lives outside us known or
Unknown, near or far.

XIII. Feed the Earth Queries

How does one feed the Earth
Which is the source of all life?

Who feeds the Earth when
the Earth is the Mother
who nourishes us all?

In which season can we
Really feed the Earth which
has its own seasonal nourishment
for seasons on end?

XIV. Spirit-Places in Our Lives

Grandma astutely said:
There are three spirit-places in our lives –
where we are born
where we are happy
where we die
and if all three stay the same,
then we are in
the best place on this earth.

Praise for Rhythms of Dignity

"Akwasi Aidoo's *Rhythms of Dignity* is a remarkable, bold first collection. There is a rich diversity in range of form, expressiveness, experience, and passion. Reading through this work is a journey through the undercurrents of experience that reflect on living through the charged realities of the 'post-colonial' decades of our modern African not only with an intimate Pan-African awareness of history but also with a poignant sensibility of brotherhood, sisterhood and belonging. Clearly evocative of the age the poet has lived through, these poems have both a sharp clear eye on history, and an abiding tender trust in human relationships."
                    – Abena P.A. Busia, Professor of literature, poet,
                              and Ghanaian ambassador to Brazil.

"Akwasi Aidoo weaves together in warm and passionate verses our timeless dreams of freedom, dignity and humanity which shall neither be deferred nor deterred regardless of what *they* say and what *their* SAPs ('sanitize African passion'!) and Davos prescribe. Enjoy the dreams of 'life and joy' that is the *Rhythms of Dignity*. Akwasi is one of Africa's foremost poets. Akwasi, you make us proud as Africans and as a part of humanity in what you sing and what you pen. May your Rhythms continue to inspire us and light the road to freedom."
                    – Issa Shivji, Emeritus Professor of Public Law &
                    First Julius Nyerere Professor of Pan-African Studies,
                              University of Dar es Salaam, Tanzania.

"Expansive and personal, Aidoo's writing carries us from intimate scenes in the doctor's office to contemplation on the African continent's fallen heroes. From Addis to Dakar then across the Atlantic, we travel with him through music, love, politics, the whole gamut of human relations. The poems read like a love letter and leave the reader with a strong dose of hope for the future."
                    – Ayesha Harruna Attah, author of *The Hundred Wells of Salaga*
                              and *The Deep Blue Between,* etc.

"Akwasi Aidoo's *Rhythms of Dignity* is that unusual of literary artefacts that combines large scale Pan-Africanist observations with the most minute attention to everyday details. There are poems here to read in quiet and reflection, some to rage to, and yet others to call out to our next door neighbor on a Sunday morning and say: 'Hear this!'"

– **Ato Quayson,** Professor of English, Stanford University, USA.

"In this collection of poems covering Africa, meditation and memory and everything in between, we hear Akwasi Aidoo's voice mingled with the voices of our ancestors, our past and our future, calling to us to reflect as 'life streaming hurriedly to us'. Woven within the lyricism of the words, the poems are a political and social commentary on life that evoke Langston Hughes and reminds us of the stories we tell and are told about us. Buy it, read it and be discomfited and comforted in turn."

– **Ayisha Osori,** Executive Director, OSIWA, and author of *Love Does Not Win Elections.*

"Akwasi Aidoo's poems in *Rhythms of Dignity* are 'dances, dreams and struggles' in verses that tread both light and heavy steps across memories, accidents and emotions twisting, swirling and twirling movements in different shapes, sizes and color. These poems croon our histories, drum our prejudices, clap our hopes and mock in lilting tones our oppression. In this collection, we have glorious offerings of multiple gifts and graces filled with different colors, sounds, tastes and scents. Here are 'rhythms' that you dance to, fight with and cry and laugh to. Only an Akwasi Aidoo with his polyvalent journeys across life's many pathways could have written them. He saw, smelled, tasted, heard, danced, laughed and cried across geographies, races, cultures, languages and times in these poems. It is a lengthy collection with plenty of spaces for the reader to come, go and come back. In the end, the reader finds what they seek both intentionally and subliminally in their dance to these rhythms."

– **Tade Akin Aina,** Executive Director, Partnership for African Social and Governance Research.